1/14

D0617975

FORENSICS IN
AMERICAN CULTURE

SOLVING CRIMES WITH SCIENCE:
Forensics

FORENSICS IN AMERICAN CULTURE

Jean Ford

Mason Crest

Mason Crest
450 Parkway Drive, Suite D
Broomall, PA 19008
www.masoncrest.com

Copyright © 2014 by Mason Crest, an imprint of National Highlights, Inc. All rights reserved. No part of this publication may be reproduced or transmitted in any form or by any means, electronic or mechanical, including photocopying, recording, taping, or any information storage and retrieval system, without permission from the publisher.

Printed and bound in the United States of America.

First printing
9 8 7 6 5 4 3 2 1

Series ISBN: 978-1-4222-2861-6
ISBN: 978-1-4222-2870-8
ebook ISBN: 978-1-4222-8956-3

The Library of Congress has cataloged the
        hardcopy format(s) as follows:

            Library of Congress Cataloging-in-Publication Data

Ford, Jean (Jean Otto)
   Forensics in American culture / Jean Ford.
      p. cm. — (Solving crimes with science, forensics)
   Audience: 012.
   Audience: Grades 7 to 8.
   Includes index.
   ISBN 978-1-4222-2870-8 (hardcover) — ISBN 978-1-4222-2861-6 (series) — ISBN 978-1-4222-8956-3
(ebook)
   1. Crime in popular culture—Juvenile literature. 2. Crime in mass media—Juvenile literature. 3. Criminal investigation in mass media—Juvenile literature. 4. Forensic sciences—Juvenile literature. I. Title.
   HV8073.8.F67 2014
   363.25—dc23
                                    2013006930

Produced by Vestal Creative Services.
www.vestalcreative.com

Contents

Introduction

By Jay A. Siegel, Ph.D.
Director, Forensic and Investigative Sciences Program
Indiana University, Purdue University, Indianapolis

It seems like every day the news brings forth another story about crime in the United States. Although the crime rate has been slowly decreasing over the past few years (due perhaps in part to the aging of the population), crime continues to be a very serious problem. Increasingly, the stories we read that involve crimes also mention the role that forensic science plays in solving serious crimes. Sensational crimes provide real examples of the power of forensic science. In recent years there has been an explosion of books, movies, and TV shows devoted to forensic science and crime investigation. The wondrously successful *CSI* TV shows have spawned a major increase in awareness of and interest in forensic science as a tool for solving crimes. *CSI* even has its own syndrome: the "*CSI* Effect," wherein jurors in real cases expect to hear testimony about science such as fingerprints, DNA, and blood spatter because they saw it on TV.

The unprecedented rise in the public's interest in forensic science has fueled demands by students and parents for more educational programs that teach the applications of science to crime. This started in colleges and universities but has filtered down to high schools and middle schools. Even elementary school students now learn how science is used in the criminal justice system. Most educators agree that this developing interest in forensic science is a good thing. It has provided an excellent opportunity to teach students science—and they have fun learning it! Forensic science is an ideal vehicle for teaching science for several reasons. It is truly multidisciplinary; practically every field of science has forensic applications. Successful forensic scientists must be good problem solvers and critical thinkers. These are critical skills that all students need to develop.

In all of this rush to implement forensic science courses in secondary schools throughout North America, the development of grade-appropriate resources that help guide students and teachers is seriously lacking. This new series: *Solving Crimes With Science: Forensics* is important and timely. Each book in the series contains a concise, age-appropriate discussion of one or more areas of forensic science.

Students are never too young to begin to learn the principles and applications of science. Forensic science provides an interesting and informative way to introduce scientific concepts in a way that grabs and holds the students' attention. *Solving Crimes With Science: Forensics* promises to be an important resource in teaching forensic science to students twelve to eighteen years old.

1

Fascination and Fear

Brad unexpectedly leaves his teaching job early one afternoon. On his way out, he tells another staff member that his friend Larry is stuck and needs a ride. No one hears from Brad again.

Brad's brother thinks Brad would never leave work just to give someone a ride. But witnesses place Brad and Larry together at a diner that day, and police find Brad's abandoned car parked outside. Larry claims that Brad left the diner with a strange woman in another car, but his story doesn't hold up when compared to testimony of other diner patrons.

Larry's wife adds to mounting concerns when she confides—based on Larry's history of violence—that she wouldn't be surprised if Larry was involved in Brad's disappearance. She clarifies, "Larry thought I was having an affair with Brad." (Brad's wife and others deny any affair.) Larry becomes the main suspect in Brad's disappearance, and police obtain a search warrant for Larry's remote camper.

What does the search yield? Not much. Someone thoroughly cleaned the camper before police got there. Yet investigators find one, tiny speck of organic matter—the size of a head of a pin—on one wall, plus one jagged bullet fragment.

Scientists identify the matter as mammal cerebellum; DNA testing isolates it as Brad's brain matter. "Soft damage" to the bullet is consistent with damage bullets sustain passing through human beings, and the caliber is the same as Larry's gun. Police arrest Larry. He is tried and convicted of Brad's murder, mostly because of that one microscopic, gray speck and one tattered shell casing.

This crime is true. It is a tale of jealousy, homicide, and science that was the subject of "Traces of Truth," a 2005 episode of Court TV's *Forensics Files*. Larry Moore murdered Brad Brisbin in West Yellowstone, Montana, and forensic science told the tale.

What Is Forensic Science?

Forensic science is simply any science applied to questions whose answers have legal ramifications. Our word "forensic" originates from the Latin word *forensis*, which literally translates "of the forum," the place where legal proceedings of ancient Rome took place. Forensic (an adjective) came to mean "connected with or pertaining to courts of law." Forensics (with an s) is the noun.

Many sciences have forensic equivalents. For example, most of us are familiar with odontology or dentistry. Forensic odontology would be the ap-

Tiny Testimonials

Insects can be valuable witnesses. When a person dies, the body begins to decay immediately, giving off odors that attract specific insects at distinct intervals. Each type of insect's activity is predictable, so bug behaviors can indicate where a victim died and under what specific environmental conditions. They can also provide the approximate time of death. If a corpse, for example, is still infested with maggots, a forensic entomologist knows that body has been dead for at least twelve hours. If maggots are present along with spiders and millipedes, then she knows the person was dead for at least forty-eight hours. Much of this knowledge was collected thanks to University of Tennessee's "Body Farm" and its founder Dr. William M. Bass III. By observing the dead bodies left to decay on the Body Farm, forensic entomologists now have rough timelines of predictable insect activity in and around dead bodies. Timelines vary with conditions like the presence of water or snow.

plication of dentistry to legal matters such as identifying a corpse through dental records or comparing bite wounds to a suspect's teeth. Entomology is the science of studying insects. *Forensic* entomology is the study of insects associated with dead bodies. If insects are present on a corpse, knowledge of those insects' habits and life cycles can estimate time of death.

Other forensic fields include forensic psychology (minds, including criminal profiling), forensic serology (blood/body fluids), forensic geology (earth/soil), forensic anthropology (skeletons/bones), forensic toxicology (drugs/poisons), forensic ballistics (firearms/bullets/gunpowder), forensic graphology (handwriting), forensic dactyloscopy (fingerprints), and even forensic art (facial reproductions based on actual skulls and anthropology), just to name a few. Clearly, career possibilities in forensic science are as varied as the crimes they seek to solve, and with the growing popularity of crime-based entertainment, they're sure to attract more and more students. (See chapter 7.)

The Forensics Fad

Why are programs such as *CSI, Forensics Files, Anatomy of a Crime,* and *Cold Case Files* so popular? Maybe because they expose processes once privy only to investigative personnel to average people—and the procedures

BODY IN OPEN AIR	INSECT ACTIVITY
10 minutes	Blowflies arrive and lay thousands of eggs in the eyes, nose, and mouth of the corpse.
12 hours	Fly eggs hatch maggots. They feed on bodily tissues.
24-36 hours	Beetles arrive. They feed on dry skin.
48 hours	Spiders, millipedes, and mites arrive. They feed on bugs already on the body.

Time line of postmortem insect activity.

intrigue us. Forensic science both fascinates and frightens. Yes, crimes still horrify, but magnetism has replaced the mystery surrounding investigative techniques; we are simultaneously disturbed and drawn.

America's evolving obsession with crime is impacting the entertainment industry and the media. With so many recent, forensics-based programs, you might think morbid curiosity is a new phenomenon. For centuries, however, humanity has demonstrated a fascination with that which frightens them.

Timeless Obsession

In Chicago, Illinois, one afternoon in May, fourteen-year-old Bobby strolls home from a neighborhood schoolyard. As the teenager walks down the street, he doesn't notice two young men shadowing him in a dark car. By nightfall the teen is dead, clubbed to death with a chisel.

Members of a railroad crew stumble upon his nude body twenty-four hours later stuffed headfirst, face down into a waterlogged *culvert* twenty miles (32 kilometers) south of the city. (A workman happened to see the boy's feet protruding from an opening in an embankment beneath the tracks.) The victim's clothes are missing, and his killers have burned away any potentially identifying features with hydrochloric acid.

Between the time of the murder and the railroad crew's discovery, Bobby's parents receive a ransom note. The author guarantees that if they meet his demands as instructed, he will return Bobby unharmed. But just as the boy's father arranges to meet the kidnappers—money in hand—he receives word that his son has been found; an uncle has just identified the body.

The media launches into a flurry of activity. Its coverage is graphic, and an engrossed city hangs on every word. Police scientists determine that an unusually intelligent typist produced the note on an Underwood typewriter, and used the press to further their investigation. The **coroner** publicly pronounces, "Only an educated person could have drafted a letter in such perfect English."

Newspapers dub the murder the "Crime of the Century" and promptly sell out. News anchors speculate on everything from motive to perpetrators; ratings soar. Largely in response to public fear and outrage, two major Chicago newspapers separately post $5,000 rewards for information leading to the arrest of the culprits. Media fascination with the crime is unprecedented. Thousands gawk as a family mourns.

Officers find a unique pair of glasses—the only evidence left at the crime scene—that leads them to the murderers. Just who were these killers? Paranoid addicts on a violent high? Sick pedophiles? What kind of person could target a child, snatch him, savagely beat him, and then mutilate his body beyond recognition? It turned out the perpetrators in this case were accomplished, eighteen- and nineteen-year-old graduate students from families of wealth and prestige.

One killer had an IQ over 160, and the other's was so high examiners couldn't measure it. (Some tests placed it at an estimated 210 to 220.) In either case, each murderer was a genius in his own right. Both had earned undergraduate degrees before their eighteenth birthdays. One was already in law school.

The randomness of the crime, the wealth and social prominence of the killers, their astounding intellect, and especially the disturbing lack of motive all contributed to a media fascination unlike any previously afforded a murder trial. When the accused's families jointly hired renowned attorney Clarence Darrow, headlines screamed, "Million-Dollar Defense!" When the defense brought in three psychiatrists, the press dubbed them "Three Wise Men from the East." Every detail of the trial became fodder for a media feeding frenzy.

The media has long exploited people's fascination with unique and morbid crime stories.

Predictably, amateur explanations of the killing shifted as the trial unfolded. In search of "why," reporters first portrayed the young men as cold, calculating psychopaths, then bored, overindulged, rich kids looking for thrills. Rumors of homosexual fascinations between the killers eventually surfaced, adding intrigue. Finally, citing separate instances of childhood abuse by the families' hired help (the nannies did it?), journalists characterized the killers as fragile, lonely victims. The public couldn't get enough.

Eventually "the movie" came out, followed years later by a second *celluloid* depiction. Various authors made small fortunes in multiple books, each spinning its own angle on the crime and motive while remaining remarkably true to known facts. The populace ate it up.

Can you guess the year, even the decade, that this crime took place? Another crime, this time in Lucan, Biddulph Township, Ontario, takes place one February night. A group of twenty to thirty men stealthily approaches the home of a rival clique, intending to settle an old score. Just twelve hours before James is to testify against this skulking pack, the mob bursts in on the man's slumbering family and slaughters everyone inside except a neighbor boy who was spending the night. (He hid when the **carnage** began.)

All four adults present—James, another man, and two women—suffer horrible deaths. The gang gouges the men's eyes, castrates, and beheads them; mob members brutalize the two women, torturing them with a red-hot iron

Crimes shatter lives as well as tangible objects.

poker before imposing similar fates. All victims are set ablaze with fuel oil, even as one of the women still breathes. But the group is not finished with its killing.

Blood-drenched, excited, and emboldened, the mob moves on to James's oldest son Will's house four miles (6.4 kilometers) away. At least twelve men approach his stoop as one shouts into the night, "Fire! Fire! Get out, Will!" A dozen **carbines** flash and roar when the first sleepy person comes to the door.

Shotgun blasts pepper Will's brother John. Blinded by the darkness, the gang unknowingly kills the wrong man and recedes into the darkness. The men think they've gotten away with murder, but Will and his wife live to tell the tale.

What happened in James's home would have remained a complete mystery if it were not for the visiting boy, who, at the first hint of danger, scurried under his bed and survived. Based on his testimony, county detectives arrest six men whom they believe orchestrated the massacre. As details pour out, the local press prints frequent updates, following the culprits' trials for over a year.

Lucan's massacre eventually makes national headlines, and Canadians want more details. The **minutiae** of any past quarrel that fueled these feuding factions pours onto newsprint. Talk about gossip! Even the *London Free Press* (based in Ontario) reports every spat: "Several thousand dollars worth of property . . . was destroyed by fire, the origin traced to incendiaries. . . . Some fifteen horses . . . perished, either by burning alive or otherwise. . . . The latest outrage caused a great deal of indignation."

The first jury **deadlocks**, and the second finds that there's not enough evidence to convict the men. Headlines scream "Not Guilty!" and the alleged murderers go free. But the story doesn't end there.

Oddly enough, a number of men suspected in the slaughter meet tragic demises. One dies after a man cuts his throat with a broken bottle; a bull gorges another; a third drowns. The press pounces on an opportunity to continue its coverage, and rumors of a "victim's curse" spread across the nation. The media and its audience loved it.

What year do you think these events transpired?

Ingredients in both these crimes are certainly modern: kidnapping, murder, child abuse, the "abuse excuse," psychopaths, pricey attorneys, expert witnesses, warring gangs, prejudice, rivalry, revenge, bloodshed, guns, grieving families longing for privacy, an intrusive press, speculating journalists, opportunistic writers, gossip, and insatiable public intrigue. Any element of these cases could be one of countless sound bites heard dozens of times per day on CNN or Court TV.

Headline Honcho

The sensational title "Crime of the Century" was not new in 1924. Its first recorded use was in an 1898 headline penned by writer Henry Hunt: "The Crime of the Century: Or the Assassination of Dr. Patrick Henry Cronin." The case to which the author referred was the brutal murder of Patrick Cronin, a Chicago physician. Members of an Irish secret society hacked the good doctor to death after he accused the group's leaders of embezzling society funds. Hunt is credited with the origin of the phrase.

Today, true crime shows and reality TV dominate television programming.

But they're not contemporary sound bites. These two crimes and the series of events that followed each of them occurred in precomputer, pre-television eras: 1924 and 1880.

Most Americans seem to think that obsession with crime is a new phenomenon. After all, media orgies, graphic reporting, and the prevalence of morbid curiosity certainly define our times. But in fact, humanity's obsession with others' dark deeds has been around for a long, long time.

Fascination and Fear   **19**

Classics

The case with which we opened this chapter was the slaying of young Bobby Franks on May 21, 1924, over ninety years ago. On trial for his murder were Nathan F. Leopold Jr. and Richard A. Loeb, two students who killed young Franks for no better reason than the thrill of killing. Even their famous lawyer Clarence Darrow stated in his summation, "Not for money, not for spite, not for hate. They killed him as they might kill a spider or a fly, for the experience." The public was simultaneously outraged and intrigued.

Think about the era in which this murder took place. Before wireless computers, DVDs, CDs, television, and for many, indoor plumbing, the only sources of news were the daily paper, the telegraph office, "silent" newsreels at theaters, the local switchboard (telephone) operator, and for a few well-to-do families, radio broadcasts. Yet somehow thousands of American citizens became obsessed with the Leopold and Loeb trial. How exactly did the masses learn of the crime—or perhaps more important, why were so many intrigued?

Now go back forty more years: preradio, prenewsreel, pretelephone, precar, even prelightbulb. The second case was Ontario's infamous "Black Donnelly" murders of 1880. Crude telegraphs, newspapers, and word-of-mouth by travelers on horseback or rail were the few means of spreading news or gossip. Yet from British Columbia to Nova Scotia, Canadians absorbed every gruesome detail of the slayings. Rumors, legends, and tales of curses spread wildly from coast to coast. Again, how and why?

The Mindset

First, the why. Clearly, fascination with human being's brutality to other humans is nothing new. Gladiator contests filled coliseums to capacity in

Dating Systems and Their Meaning

You might be accustomed to seeing dates expressed with the abbreviations BC or AD, as in the year 1000 BC or the year AD 1900. For centuries, this dating system has been the most common in the Western world. However, since BC and AD are based on Christianity (BC stands for Before Christ and AD stands for anno Domini, Latin for "in the year of our Lord"), many people now prefer to use abbreviations that people from all religions can be comfortable using. The abbreviations BCE (meaning Before Common Era) and CE (meaning Common Era) mark time in the same way (for example, 1000 BC is the same year as 1000 BCE, and AD 1900 is the same year as 1900 CE), but bce and ce do not have the same religious overtones as BC and AD.

ancient Rome. In the first century CE, public crucifixion, flogging, and stoning attracted massive, taunting crowds. These gruesome displays were all legal, actually encouraged—if not mandated—by law, and embraced as entertainment. People went to see other human beings eaten by lions or killed in some other gruesome way, just as simply as today's North Americans might go to a football or hockey game.

When we move ahead one thousand years, we find the widespread use of public stocks depended on gawking passersby to further humiliate prisoners. Trials drew young and old alike. Entire communities held picnics at public hangings, many cheering as doors dropped out beneath

Before television and radio, novels often incorporated tidbits of real crimes into their stories.

the condemned. Long before Laci Peterson and O. J. Simpson, "crime and punishment" was a spectator sport. But this morbid fascination with others' suffering isn't the only reason why people are obsessed with crimes.

People are curious by nature. Puzzle-solving is innately human. Give us a mystery to solve, and most of us are intrigued. We love to play detective—and crimes often present us with our greatest mysteries.

Archaic Means

If geography in earlier times confined firsthand accounts of crime to local areas, how did the details leak into the collective conscience of an entire nation or people? Even more astounding, how could they spread throughout the pre-TV, preradio, pretelegraph world? In less technological eras, people depended on word-of-mouth and the written word.

As a genre, most literary experts agree that "true crime" reporting has been around since the late 1800s. A precursor to the nonfiction best seller of today, fiction authors such as Wilkie Collins and Charles Dickens often incorporated incidents and characters from actual crimes into their works. For example, Collins applied details from the 1860 "Road House" case to his novel *The Moonstone*. Charles Dickens utilized bona fide offenses in *Oliver Twist*, among other titles.

But before accounts of real crimes appeared even in novel form, there were simpler ways to spread details of particularly shocking crimes throughout entire regions. From the sixteenth to the nineteenth centuries, plays often presented the gory details. Shakespeare's *Julius Caesar* and *Henry VIII* are examples of such crime-based plays.

In preindustrialized America, "broadsheet ballads" were common conveyors of murder and mayhem. Publishers printed the ballads on thin sheets of paper, and street salesmen hocked them for a penny or less, making them accessible to nearly everyone. These "rags" frequently omitted

The Newgate Calendar began as a monthly list of those in jail and their offenses. Deputies compiled the names on long sheets of parchment and posted them for locals to see. This list evolved to include deathbed confessions and details of the crimes. One deputy from a jail in Newgate, England, started the practice, hence its name. This practice immigrated to America with colonials.

authors' names, so accountability for accuracy was rare. Subject matter varied as widely as popular interest: politics, religion, social reform, crime, and even sex. Sensationalism was the norm.

Broadsheet ballads were as much about entertainment as information. No subject was off limits. Infamous American examples from the nineteenth century include ballads detailing the brutal slayings of two young girls, Blanche Lamont and Minnie Williams, in San Francisco in 1820, Sarah Cornwell's murder in 1833, the kidnapping of little Charles Brewster Ross near Philadelphia in 1874, and the murders of Lizzie Borden's parents in Fall River, Massachusetts, in 1873.

Less commonly, perpetrators provided accounts of their handiwork in publications containing convicts' confessions. Sometimes editors would adapt these confessions to moralistic crime stories, such as those that appear in the 1773 *Newgate Calendar*.

The most familiar archaic mass communication tool is also the most childlike: the rhyme. Childlike rhymes had broad appeal in Europe and North America among both the peasantry and the privileged. Even the illiterate easily understood, easily recalled, and easily shared the morbid tales. People readily accepted them as fact and folklore.

The small New England town of Fall River spawned perhaps the most infamous of such rhymes. Late in nineteenth-century Massachusetts, Elizabeth Borden was the prime suspect in the gruesome axe murders of her

According to literary historians, the child's rhyme "Jack and Jill" retold the tale of the 1793 beheadings of Louis XVI ("lost his crown") and his queen, Marie Antoinette ("came tumbling after"). It first appeared in villages in France in 1795.

FORENSICS IN AMERICAN CULTURE

stepmother and father. She was eventually tried and acquitted, but suspicions of guilt followed her the rest of her days. Details of the killings made their way throughout much of America, despite limited communication and transportation systems.

> Lizzy Borden took an axe
> and gave her mother forty whacks.
> When she saw what she had done,
> she gave her father forty-one.

The rhyme was chanted in schoolyards across America. Even little children knew about Lizzie.

Clearly, **aberrant** criminal acts and people's fascination with the details are as old as human civilization. Whether via newspapers, books, rhymes, plays, or gossip, people have always found a way to peer into—and **vicariously** share—the violence that frightens them.

So what's changed? Why are twenty-first century Americans seemingly more obsessed with crime than previous generations?

Our Changing Judicature

One factor could be the evolution of our justice system. Over the last four hundred years, the judicial process in Europe and America gradually shifted from one based on guilt, degradation, torture, and confession to one centered on trial by evidence. Previously, courts assumed guilt, and the accused had to prove his innocence, whereas now the accused is "innocent until proven guilty."

This shift added a series of procedures never previously required in judicature: searching for and examining physical evidence, fact finding, observing the accused, interviewing witnesses, inquests, and holding trials where both sides presented arguments and displayed evidence. Suddenly, law enforcement needed a new breed of personnel: the detective. These sleuths fascinated and, at times, amazed onlookers in the courtroom, often demystifying the previously unexplainable. News accounts spread details of their work, forever hooking the public.

Modern Means

Another factor may simply be the time in which we live. Are we really any more obsessed with violence—or are we simply more aware of the tendency?

As advances in technology changed the way information is reported and received, the popular media realized an unprecedented ability to reach national and even international audiences. The curious no longer needed broadsheet ballads or the town gossip. Computers, satellites, microchips,

The flashing lights of police cars and emergency vehicles often draw a fascinated crowd.

the Internet, telecommunications, and advances in printing, transportation, and distribution transformed cities, states, provinces, nations, continents, and ultimately the world into the local town square. Literally millions could hear, read, or see a crime report instantly and simultaneously.

Stiff competition grew within the news community as broadcasters vied for greater audience shares. Being first "on location" or obtaining "exclusive" coverage became critical to increasing viewers, readership, and ratings. Seeking that edge, magazine photographs gradually became more graphic; newspapers went to color photos; radio and television broadcasts were more frequently "live." Each medium had to outdo the other to draw larger audiences.

Sensational Profits

TV and radio differ from print in that their stories are not "sold" like those offered in books, newspapers, or magazines. Instead networks rely on advertising sales to make money.

Companies advertise products and services during the programs we watch. These companies want the most people possible to see and hear their ads. Consequently, networks charge more to broadcast ads during the most popular programs. For example, a thirty-second commercial shown during *CSI* or *Law & Order* might cost four times that of one aired during a less popular show or time slot. The more popular a program is the more people who watch it; and the more people who watch it, the more people who see its ads. Greater numbers of viewers equal more potential sales, so advertisers are willing to pay huge sums of money for the exposure.

To stay competitive—to keep and attract advertising revenues—each medium had to find means of outdoing its competition. Consequently, the

Pricey Promotions

The most expensive advertising in television airs on Super Bowl Sunday, and it gets more expensive each year. Yet advertisers line up annually for their spots.

Year	Cost per Thirty-second Commercial
1967 Super Bowl	$42,000.00
1995 Super Bowl	$1 million
2001 Super Bowl	$2 million
2004 Super Bowl	$2.3 million
2013 Super Bowl	$4 million

(Source: The Associated Press)

general public found themselves faced with increasingly shocking crime coverage. What once only perpetrators, law enforcement, and crime-scene investigators saw, networks openly transmitted to average living rooms. The curious and concerned could watch crimes and subsequent trials as actual events unfolded—and in astonishing detail.

Why *do* we watch? For the same reason morose rhymes, ballads, gossip, and folk tales spread like wildfire from coast to coast in the 1800s: shock value. Most of us like the rush we get from being scared or even repulsed *when we know we are safe.* Isn't that what campfire tales are all about?

Whether fear, compassion, harbored aggression, or simple intrigue drives human interest in such things, humanity is morbidly curious, and the more dramatically a source can feed that curiosity, the greater its audience. Something troubling and unique, though, pervades the current climate.

Avenues at our disposal to satisfy fascination with the **macabre** are countless. Affordable, convenient, and accessible images and information have rendered traditional control mechanisms ineffective. Whereas strictly regulated accessibility to such information previously deterred laypeople from seeking and seeing crime's intricacies, fewer barriers exist today.

Consequently, contemporary forms of mass communication and entertainment (TV, news media and print, movies, the Internet, etc.) are incorporating increasingly violent depictions of crime and increasingly graphic investigations to inform, engage, and amuse.

How do writers and producers create these productions? Are fictional depictions of crime, forensic investigation, and trials accurate? What about "true crime" programs? What impact has our obsession had on career options? Do we romanticize crime, or even dignify it? Where does the news media fit in?

communication

media
digital

24hours

INVES

2

Willing Witnesses: Crime and the News Media

On June 17, 1994, a white Ford Bronco crept along an interstate, black-and-whites hemming it in. The procession resembled a police escort, but this was no escort. Officers suspected one of two men in the car of killing his former wife and her male friend, and the two men were fleeing arrest. Additionally, the suspect had a gun and was threatening to kill himself. Every major network interrupted regular programming to provide live coverage of perhaps the slowest and most bizarre police chase in history.

According to CNN, an estimated 95 million viewers tuned in to watch the unfolding events of O. J. Simpson's hours-long flight from LAPD officers. (Friend Al Cowlings was at the wheel.) As word of the chase spread, hundreds of fans swarmed overpasses or lined streets to catch a glimpse of the passing vehicles. Some onlookers even sported signs encouraging O. J. to flee, while others prompted his surrender. Sixteen months later, over 100 million viewers tuned in for the live verdict.

What made these events so gripping? What characteristics of this particular crime drove news directors to focus so intensely on it? The most important factor was likely the suspect's celebrity; the accused was a former football star and an actor. Another possible factor—one that did arise at trial—was the fact that the suspect and victims were different races. Whatever the cause, the news media had—and still has—enormous power to influence the importance the public places on specific crimes.

O. J. Simpson's mug shot

In the murders of Nicole Brown Simpson and Ron Goldman, news crews clearly provided excessive coverage. Homes across the world were flooded with each detail of the case, from the initial car chase to gory images of the crime scene to moment-by-moment trial footage. As a result, many viewers felt that the trial's outcome was somehow vital. But was it really?

How many other murders, even double murders or cross-racial murders, took place during the months the Simpson trial mesmerized us? The number in America alone is in the thousands, and those victims died without a media frenzy. So why was this crime so important to so many people?

In their book *Crimes of the Century*, Gilbert Geis and Leigh B. Bienen theorize that what elevates an ordinary crime to an extraordinary one is found in the common ingredients of previous infamous crimes. They researched five twentieth-century cases that ignited media frenzies in their time: Leopold and Loeb (murder, 1924), the Scottsboro Boys (gang rape, 1931), Bruno Hauptmann (kidnapping and murder, 1932), Alger Hiss (espionage and perjury, 1948), and O. J. Simpson (murder, 1994). What did these authors conclude? The era, the character of offenders or victims, and the details of the offense could each potentially impact media coverage. In a commentary on the Leopold-Loeb case, the New York Times added two more: emotional and intellectual force.

Clearly, a crime must be universally offensive to make headlines, but the crime itself is not enough to impact a case's prominence. Horrible murders, even those of children, happen all the time, and we never hear about them. But throw in a particularly innocent victim (like the baby boy in the Hauptmann case), unlikely suspects or a puzzling motive (like Leopold-Loeb), a gruesome killing (like Simpson), or the race card in a racially tense era (like the Scottsboro case), and suddenly a crime is newsworthy. That coverage impacts the importance people place on the events.

Willing Witnesses: Crime and the News Media

CASE STUDY:
TEN-YEAR-OLD HOLLY JONES

One early evening in spring 2003, the day after Mother's Day, a ten-year-old Toronto girl tells her parents she's going to walk her friend the couple of blocks back to her house. The path is the same one she takes every day to school, so Mom and Dad aren't worried. Hours pass, and by nightfall Holly Jones hasn't come home. The night wears into morning, and mounting concerns turn into fear.

Just hours later, two bags wash up on Toronto's waterfront. Inside are Holly's remains. (Someone had sexually assaulted the little girl, murdered her, and dumped the bagged remains of her dismembered body into Lake Ontario.) What follows becomes one of the largest manhunts in Toronto's history, and the news media plays an important role. Six weeks later, police make an arrest.

This case exemplifies characteristics that elevate a crime in the media's conscience. The nature of the victim (a child), the nature of the crime (sexual assault, murder, dismemberment), and the nature of the suspect (a computer software developer) each contributed unsettling aspects that intrigued people. And the whodunit factor touched the detective in most everyone.

Here is a timeline of the events. Notice how often the news media are involved.

May 12, 2003: Holly Jones, ten, disappears. Police broadcast an "Amber Alert" to no avail.

May 13: Holly's parents, Maria Jones and George Stonehouse, appear on the news to plead for their child's return. Just hours later, a young girl's body parts, contained in two bags, wash up on the Lake Ontario shores of Toronto Island.

May 14: Investigators release photos of dumbbells police divers recovered in the lake plus photos of the two bags to the press.

May 16: Police ask the public for help identifying two men spotted on ferries near the island where Holly's remains washed ashore.

May 18: Police release additional photos of Holly, hoping to jump-start someone's memory.

May 19: Toronto police announce that the hotline has gotten 1,650-plus tips and ask for the public's continued help.

June 2: A man tries to lure a little boy out of a grocery store in Holly's neighborhood. The man takes off when the boy's mother starts screaming.

June 5: Police release yet another picture of Holly in the clothes she was wearing the day she disappeared. Police also suggest to reporters that the killer may live in the vicinity of Holly's home.

June 9: Neighborhood residents begin patrolling streets after a man boldly grabs an eight-year-old's wrist as she is walking with her mother.

June 10: Holly's school adds additional security measures after news reports of more attempted abductions in the area.

June 20: Police arrest Michael Briere, thirty-five, a software developer. Officers take him into custody at a west-end address near Holly's home. They charge him with first-degree murder. He's held without bail.

May 2004: Briere waves his right to a preliminary hearing. Rumors fly, and the press speculates he will plead guilty.

June 2004: Michael Briere pleads guilty to the first-degree murder of Holly Jones. The court imposes an automatic life sentence with no chance of parole for twenty-five years. As part of the plea, Briere explains to the court that desire consumed him after viewing child pornography, so he abducted Holly, had his way, and murdered her.

Look at JonBenét Ramsey, a six-year old child beauty pageant star found murdered in 1996. How many children are killed every day without capturing the media's attention? Why was the Ramsey case different? Like Holly Jones (see sidebar, page 34), JonBenét was a beautiful little girl. But in her case, the fact that she was a child beauty contestant, that her parents were initial suspects, and the mystery and problem of motive each contributed to its rise in media coverage.

Media Influence
and the Search for Truth

The power the press wields over people is astonishing. Sometimes that power assists the search for truth.

Headlines can influence the way the public perceives a news story.

In 1991, a Canadian jury found James Driskell guilty of the 1990 murder of Perry Dean Harder and sentenced the Manitoba man to life. From day one, controversy surrounded the validity of crucial evidence, and for twelve years, Driskell languished behind bars, maintaining his innocence. According to the CBC (Canadian Broadcasting Corporation), the case caught the attention of the *Winnipeg Free Press*, and the Association in Defense of the Wrongly Convicted took up his case largely because of its coverage.

In 2003, a judge granted Driskell bail while the Justice Department reopened the case. He was eventually cleared. Reporter Dan Lett of the *Winnipeg Free Press* won the country's coveted National Newspaper Award (NNA) in investigative reporting for his work on the story that helped free an innocent man. In this case, the press leveraged its strength to get at the truth.

Willing Witnesses: Crime and the News Media

Unfortunately, sometimes media influence gets in truth's way.

Take, for example, the case of Richard Jewell. Investigators suspected Jewell of the July 27 bombing of Olympic Park during the 1996 Olympics in Atlanta, Georgia. One woman was killed and more than a hundred were injured.

Already covering the Olympics, news crews were right there when the bomb went off. Networks repeatedly aired the scenes of chaos, and the frightening images fueled public outrage. The world wanted its culprit.

For a number of reasons, Jewell, a security guard working at the Olympics, initially became the focus of the investigation. The *Atlanta Journal-Constitution* was the first to report it, but national news agencies immediately picked up the story. For months, Richard Jewell's face graced our nightly news programs, magazine covers, and newspapers. Most people wrongly assumed he was the bomber. The government cleared Jewell of any involvement on October 26, nearly three months after the tragic events, but the damage was already done. Jewell's reputation was irreparably tarnished. His health, family, and job suffered greatly.

What went wrong in this crime coverage? Speculation. The news media prematurely cast its vote and swayed millions. The problem is that once a news medium reports a story, folks tend to believe it, and the news can't be taken back. Millions of people believed Jewell was guilty simply because that's what they heard on the news; obviously, many reporters already thought Jewell was guilty simply because authorities were questioning him.

NBC anchorman Tom Brokaw said on air before Richard Jewell was even an official suspect: "Look, they probably got enough to arrest him. They probably have got enough to try him." That's speculation, not reporting. (According to the *Wall Street Journal*, those words cost NBC $500,000 in a lawsuit Jewell later brought against the network.)

Does Violence Breed Violence?

Sometimes the amount of attention the media gives to violent crimes can actually lead to more crimes. Look at the case of Rodney King. Los Angeles Anglo-American police officers brutally beat King, an African American, during his arrest. One onlooker captured the events on home video and turned it over to newscasters. Networks replayed only the most disturbing segments countless times for the world to see.

When a jury found officers charged in the beating not guilty, race riots broke out in Los Angeles. Another amateur videographer captured the mayhem, including the frenzied pummeling of a truck driver whom rioters

Many newspapers operate under the principle that stories involving violent crime should be printed on the front page.

dragged from his cab, then stomped, kicked, and beat. The coverage was just as shocking as the King video.

Did excessive airing of King's beating fuel these subsequent riots? Did our news media's coverage of the crime whip an already tense city into a fury? If Los Angeles residents hadn't seen the video of King's beating over and over again, would they have responded with such violence to the verdicts? We'll never know.

What we do know is that news media can influence the public's reaction to a crime based on what it chooses to include (or not include) in its coverage. Sometimes viewers don't get the whole story. Whether working for newspapers, magazines, or television, reporters look for the most unusual and sensational angle for the story. If they're going to get viewers' attention, reporters need to make their stories stand out.

Since the Vietnam War, war footage has been broadcast on nightly news networks.

While some national news channels, newspapers, and primetime news broadcasts publish biased, sensational stories, not all media outlets are governed by the "if it bleeds, it leads" principle. National Public Radio (NPR) is a not-for-profit collective of independently run radio stations that air "noncommercial" news, talk, and entertainment programming. NPR affiliates operate according to a strict ethical code that requires them to be fair, honest, accurate, and unbiased in their coverage of local, national, and international news. Similarly, the Public Broadcasting Service (PBS) is a member-driven nonprofit television network that offers educational programming in 99 percent of American homes. The Independent Media Center is another group of news broadcasters that strives to cover specific issues that affect the communities they serve without corporate biases.

Because these organizations are supported by their viewers and don't rely on advertiser dollars to stay in business, they can deliver poignant, informative news and analysis without sensational headlines and slanted views. More important, these media outlets exist to enrich the lives of their audiences.

"If It Bleeds, It Leads"

On any given day, pick up a newspaper or turn to a news program and you'll learn what crimes have taken place in the world. Add extreme violence to any of them and they're sure to make headlines. The old newspaper adage "if it bleeds, it leads" illustrates the weight some media places on violent crime. The shock value draws audiences, and that means more advertising dollars.

The amount of violent crime in the news today far exceeds that of our parents' and grandparents' times. In the first half of the twentieth century, radios and black-and-white newspapers carried most of the news. The few images people encountered were still and colorless.

During the Vietnam War, through the magic of television, news crews "on location" broadcast color, moving war images into people's homes, earning the conflict the nickname the "Living Room War." Civilians of all ages, cultures, and backgrounds witnessed horrors of war for the first time. President Lyndon Johnson knew the importance of media coverage of the war. When venerable CBS news anchor Walter Cronkite questioned the war, Johnson is reported to have said, "If I've lost Cronkite, I've lost middle America." Ratings soared, and broadcast journalism has never been the same. Today you can't get the news without encountering some type of violent crime.

Cause and Effect

Media depictions of violent crime affect us whether or not we are aware of it. These effects can include **desensitization**, wanting more, fear, **stereotyping**, sympathy, and sometimes, imitation. When people see images of violence over and over again, especially real images of violent crime, the events eventually shock them less. New images are nothing they haven't seen before, so they're less disturbed by them. Witnessing violent crime repeatedly desensitizes viewers to it.

Some people love the sensation of being horrified or outraged. The thrill for them is feeling. Such excitement can become addicting, and viewers like this frequently desire more. The problem lies in that such people often need increasing intensity to get the same rush.

Our media's depiction of crime can also trigger fear. Some viewers may start to believe that crime—particularly violent crime—is more common and

CASE STUDY: BOSTON, 1962–1964

A serial killer murders at least eleven single, respectable, Boston women by strangling each of them with articles of clothing. He kills all eleven in their own apartments after sexually molesting them. The news media reports every detail of the lurid crimes and the law-abiding victims. Journalists see a pattern to the murders and dub the killer "The Boston Strangler." Women won't go out alone, and companies with night shifts see a sudden rise in absenteeism. The public is terrified, and a city holds its collective breath for nearly two years.

random than it is. Criminal acts and investigations saturate every form of news and entertainment we encounter, including video games, novels, and comic books. Marketers know crime sells, but that doesn't mean every alley harbors a rapist or your neighbor is a serial killer.

Media coverage of newsworthy crimes can also encourage stereotypes. If you doubt it, try to name two Arab criminals from recent headlines. Now name two Arab heroes who recently made network news because of the good they're doing in their communities. Those Arab heroes exist—but no matter how free of prejudice we pride ourselves on being, we don't know the heroes' names, and our thinking about a group of people is unavoidably skewed.

CASE STUDY: 1932–1934, SYMPATHETIC VILLAINS

A couple of young, Southern, impoverished lovers captivate the media as they terrorize banks and store owners in five states during a violent, two-year crime spree. They're passionate and reckless. Fully expecting to die, they will do anything—from robbery to murder—to climb out of the poverty they detest.

Who is this couple? Bonnie Parker and Clyde Barrow. Their murderous spree ends in a deadly shootout with law enforcement; bullets riddle their famous car and their bodies.

Every human being has strong biases, including reporters. Balanced, objective coverage by the news media is more the exception than the norm. That fact is important to remember.

Look at the case of Sacco and Vanzetti. Many people believe the two men were victims of an era's stereotypes. Their communist beliefs were widely unpopular in the twenties, and the media played into the public's fear of communism. *That* became the focus of the 1921 trial instead of any evidence (or lack thereof) that they had murdered two men in South Braintree, Massachusetts. Most historians today agree that these men were innocent of the murder charges of which the jury convicted them; they might have died in the electric chair for their political convictions alone.

Not only can the news media perpetuate and magnify stereotypes, it can also create sympathy for those who don't deserve it. Look at Bonnie

Violence enters living rooms by way of television sets across North America.

and Clyde. These two criminals became public folk heroes during their early-1930s crime spree, largely due to press coverage. News reporters romanticized the pair, creating sympathy across Depression-ravaged communities. A downcast world needed someone to cheer. Some towns actually applauded the media-created Robin Hoods as they drove through, and others even offered to harbor the fugitives for a time. This couple brutally murdered other human beings—but because of the way they were portrayed in the news, Americans loved Bonnie and Clyde.

Willing Witnesses: Crime and the News Media

Bonnie Parker and Clyde Barrow

Occasionally, someone does try to imitate something he sees in the media, but such a direct cause-and-effect link is rare. Thankfully, most people don't imitate crimes the media depicts.

Truth or Consequences

News reports depict powerful stories—but what editors choose to include or not include can mislead viewers. Nightly newscasts can *sterilize* crime and grossly simplify it. They routinely air chalk-outlined bloodstains on city sidewalks or a bruised victim telling her tale from her hospital bed. Unless the crime is "sensational" (like the Simpson/Goldman and Peterson murders), the news will neglect to follow up the story. Failing to include the long-term consequences for both victimizer and victim is a distortion of reality.

For example, what happens to suspects after we see officers take them away, arms handcuffed behind their backs, hiding their heads in the back-seat of a police car, or on a "perp" walk? Are they convicted—or did police nab the wrong person? What happens to the perpetrators in prison—do they become victims themselves? What about the effects of their crimes on their family members and relationships? Do nightmares ever plague them? Do they repeat-offend? When someone resorts to crime to solve a problem—whether they planned to or not—do the issues really end as tidily as the media indicates, or does choosing to break the law create a host of new problems no one ever considers?

Expanding Fascination

You'd think we would have had enough. Doesn't the amount of "bad news" in papers, in magazines, on radio, and on TV provide ample fodder for our crime-craving appetites? Apparently not. Entertainment programming on television is the latest outlet for our obsession.

3

Armchair Investigators: Crime on Television

The detective purposefully sets his partner's revolver and the large rock to which it's tethered on the bridge railing. "Your theory, though admirable in psychology, did not quite adhere to the facts." He demonstrates by pushing the small boulder off the railing to waters below while holding the still attached gun. The rope uncoils under the rock's weight, pulls taut, and our sleuth raises the resisting revolver to his right temple.

"For all your deductions about Gibson being the perpetrator of the crime, substitute his wife; that it was she who took the twin pistols from the gun room, she who fired a single round . . . and placed that gun in Miss Dunbar's wardrobe." He pauses, then concludes to himself, "Cold, crafty, premeditated . . . down to the last detail."

The detective suddenly pretends to fire a single, suicidal shot to his temple and immediately releases the revolver. It violently rips from his hand, its tether yanking it toward the river. The weapon strikes the stone handrail with such force that it chips it as it whips over the edge and plunges into the water. This new nick duplicates one next to it, the one left on the underside of the railing at the time of death. "Ah, inevitable . . . an exact demonstration."

After dredging the river for the demo gun, rope, and rock, police snare an identical contraption made, of course, with the missing gun tied to another rock using a similar length of rope. This evidence clinches the accused's innocence. Sherlock Holmes sums up the shooting victim, "A vindictive woman, passionate, unbalanced."

Dr. Watson finishes the thought: "disguising her own crime [suicide] and falsifying a charge of murder upon an innocent victim."

This scene is from "The Problem with Thor Bridge," an episode of Granada TV's *Casebook of Sherlock Holmes*. The super sleuth has just solved another crime by exposing a murder for the malicious suicide it was. What was the pivotal evidence?

Police inspectors never noticed a small chip in the underside of the bridge's railing, but Holmes did. Why? This detective had spent years honing his observation skills and scientific knowledge. He was arguably the greatest detective who ever lived—but he existed only in an author's mind.

Little did Sir Arthur Conan Doyle know his Sherlock Holmes was years ahead of his time. Today's investigative tools are certainly more advanced, but a hundred years after delighted readers first encountered his genius, Holmes's methods remain essentially unchanged: appreciating seemingly

Elementary, Dear Watson

Sir Arthur Conan Doyle introduced Sherlock Holmes in 1887 in his novel *A Study in Scarlet*. Holmes was among the first protagonists to solve crimes scientifically, relying on forensic evidence. The detective could tell how many men were at a crime scene by cigar stubs in the fireplace; from what part of town a man came by the mud on his boots; and even a gentleman's profession by the kind of cane he carried. Holmes's intellect amazed subsequent generations in more novels, then film, and he eventually surged in popularity in the 1980s when public television aired Granada TV Productions' series *The Casebook of Sherlock Holmes*. He hit the big screen more recently in films in 2009 and 2011.

insignificant clues, applying impeccable logic to scientific knowledge, and keen observation. The process still amazes us.

Pick up any *TV Guide* or local program guide in any newspaper. Dozens of crime-related programs air every day, and that's just during prime time. From investigative series like Crime Stories to true-crime movies like *The Perfect Husband* (2004), from countless fictional series like *CSI* to educational programming like *Nova* or *Nature*, from TV magazines like *Prime Time* to twenty-four-hour news networks like CNN and MSNBC or even live coverage from Court TV, America's obsession with crime is easily satisfied.

True Crime Shows

Television series like *Anatomy of a Crime*, *Forensic Files*, *Cold Case Files*, *Crime Stories*, *Investigative Reports*, *FBI Files*, *True Detectives*, *The Investigators*, and *City Confidential* afford us windows into actual crimes and the investigations that follow them. These accounts are not fictional. The crimes, the victims, the suspects, the families, the witnesses, the detectives, the evidence, and the forensic procedures are all too real.

What editors choose to include in these programs—not everything can be aired on television—is often startling, graphic, and usually quite accurate despite obvious limitations. Real-life witnesses, investigators, crime-scene photos, transcripts, 911 telephone recordings, and security videos spare us no detail. Their content can be as horrifying as it is real. And we're simultaneously repulsed and absorbed.

Self-Policing

The television industry created its own rating system to alert viewers to the content of shows before they watch them. Ratings appear in the upper-left corner of the TV screen as each program begins. (Television guides also list most ratings.) News and sports are not rated.

TVY	Children of all ages
TVY7	Children seven or older (mild violence)

TVG   General audiences
(little or no sex,
violence, or profanity)

TVPG Parental guidance ad-
vised for children
under seven (mild sex,
violence, or profanity)

TV14 Parental guidance ad-
vised for children
under fourteen (moder-
ate sex, violence, or
profanity)

TVMA Mature audiences only
(graphic violence, sex,
or profanity)

The rating system also includes "footnotes" to further clarify content. They are:

D Suggestive dialogue
L Coarse language
S Sexual content
V Violence
FV Fantasy violence.

Fictional Series

CSI, *CSI Miami*, *CSI NY*, *Law & Order*, *Law & Order SVU*, *Law & Order Criminal Intent*, *The Practice*, *NYPD Blue*, *Cold Case*, *Crossing Jordan*, *Diagnosis Murder*, *Monk*, *Murder She Wrote*, *Mystery*, *The Medium*, *Bones*, and *Dexter* all offer glimpses into the world of forensic detection, too. (This is just a partial list of what's on television!) The plots and characters are fictional, but many shows in this genre strive for realism.

For example, some writers loosely draw storylines from actual crimes in the news. *Law & Order* has frequently ripped plots from headlines: an infamous New York psychiatrist is charged with his child's murder and spousal-abuse; a 1970s activist is the prime suspect in his girlfriend's twenty-year-old murder; a baby boy dies in the care of his foreign nanny; a patient accuses her gynecologist of raping her during an exam. Using news stories to construct more authentic story lines has endless potential.

The Envelope Please

In 2001, Court TV conducted a national poll jointly with *American Police Beat* magazine, one of the largest and most widely read publications by law enforcement officers. The subject: justice-related television dramas. More than one thousand subscribers of the magazine, primarily police officers, responded to the poll. Officers overwhelmingly felt that news coverage and documentaries of police activity make their job more difficult. They also thought realism was the most important aspect of police dramas (over plot, action, and acting).

Crime-Solver

Perry Mason was one of the first courtroom dramas to hit TV screens. Mason, played by Raymond Burr, was a defense attorney who used his team to track evidence exonerating his clients. Each episode's climax took place in the courtroom as Mason dramatically revealed the true culprit and the forensic evidence that clinched his guilt. The plots and acting were unrealistically melodramatic, exactly what producers intended. Their goal was to grab viewers. It worked. The series was hugely popular in the late 1950s and '60s and ran for years.

Other series include well-established investigative techniques to add realism. Today, police, medical examiners, detectives, criminalists, forensic scientists, and lab technicians work collaboratively to solve a case, yet most TV crime-solvers begin as the solitary Holmes did—with simple observation.

The year 1976 introduced the first program to detail forensic science: *Quincy*. Each episode shadowed a crusading Los Angeles medical examiner as he solved puzzling death cases. Dr. Quincy, played by Jack Klugman, performed multiple duties in his quest for truth: he was a medical doctor, a coroner, a forensic investigator, and a police detective. That's where the show broke from reality.

In actuality, police departments and medical examiners' offices in cities like Los Angeles function quite separately, although cooperatively. The line of demarcation between the two is clear: medical examiners determine

Manner of Death

Medical examiners like Dr. Quincy (Quincy) or Dr. Cavanaugh (Crossing Jordan) can attribute death to one of five causes:

- Natural
- Accidental
- Suicide
- Homicide
- Undetermined

cause and estimate time of death; police officials find out who did it and why (the how overlaps). Quincy inevitably managed to see something no one else from either school noticed, but depictions of the science he used were minimal and simplistic. In that sense, the show was definitely not true to life, but viewers loved it. It was an immediate hit and ran for eight seasons.

How accurate are current fictional crime shows? We've come a long way since *Perry Mason*, but a sixty-minute episode simply doesn't have time to portray the complexities and Herculean effort inherent to forensic investigation. Producers grossly simplify forensic processes, and viewers often only see the "ah-hah!" moments. For instance, in cases involving fiber evidence, in the real world one technician often microscopically compares a known sample against literally hundreds, if not thousands of fibers one at a time. That painstaking process takes weeks, even months to complete in actual labs, not the thirty seconds a program depicts when the scientist reveals what she's discovered.

Television dramas simply can't portray the extensive work behind forensic scientists' conclusions. They don't have time, and frankly, such work can be tedious, slow, and boring—definitely not the stuff that makes good action sequences. Yet much of what producers *do* show is remarkably accurate today.

Take *CSI* for example. Extensive application of various sciences, observation, and analysis make up the three-legged stool on which real forensics thrives. All three legs appear in almost every episode. In "Blood Drops" (episode 107, the first season's seventh episode), a murderer slaughters four members of one family in their home. Lead crime-scene investigator Gil

Television crime dramas strive to portray accurate characterizations of forensic science investigations.

Grissom first notices a strong copper smell as he goes up the steps to the crime scene. Translation: lots of blood is up there. Downstairs, Grissom notices one open, kitchen drawer, and only one knife is gone. Translation: the killer knew where the knives were.

Outside, another investigator notices fresh, motorized scooter tracks in a garden near the entrance. He makes a plaster cast of the tread prints, and photographs them. Translation: it's probably the perpetrator's means of transportation. A third investigator discovers a fresh, hand-rolled cigarette butt in nearby foliage. He gathers it for later analysis. Translation: the perp (short for perpetrator) smokes and rolls his own cigarettes.

Then there's blood spatter. "It never lies," asserts Grissom. The shape of the droplets and the direction of the spattering reveal that one victim, the father, had been *exiting* his little girl's room when he was stabbed, not entering it to protect her as originally thought. This clue ultimately led to the discovery that the dad was molesting his daughter, and someone murdered him to protect her.

Observation: it's critical, but that's only the first leg of the stool, and it's useless without the other two, analysis and knowledge of forensic science. In this episode alone technicians gather, examine, and analyze wounds, blood, blood spatter, bodies, tire treads, cigarette stubs, clothing stains, footprints (lifted from linoleum with an electrostatic dust print lifter), and body fluids. Think of the number of forensic sciences involved. Imagine the varieties of analysis! Both elements are essential to interpreting observation. This is where *CSI* succeeds.

But if *CSI*'s setting is really the Las Vegas Crime Scene Unit, a large city would likely have substantial investigative facilities. Yes, urban police officials would typically reserve crime scenes for specialists in crime-scene investigation (CSIs), but the lead detective would call them in—he would be in charge of the crime scene—and CSIs would commonly spend most of

The First on the Scene

- police officers
- police detectives
- coroner
- medical examiner
- crime-scene investigation unit
- crime-scene photographer/ artists

The Criminalists

- latent print examiners
- trace evidence examiners
- tool mark examiners
- firearms examiners
- ballistics experts

The Scientists

- forensic anthropologists (bones)
- forensic accountants (finances)

- forensic botanists (plants)
- forensic chemists (substances)
- forensic criminologists (minds)
- forensic dactyloscopists (prints)
- forensic entomologists (bugs)
- forensic geologists (soils)
- forensic linguists (words)
- forensic odontologists (teeth)
- forensic pathologists (disease and injury)
- forensic profilers (characteristics and behavior)
- forensic psychiatrists (sanity, mental competence, motive)
- forensic serologists (body fluids)
- forensic toxicologists (drugs and poisons)

their time just collecting, documenting, and transporting evidence, nothing more. Additional specialized personnel (lab technicians, forensic scientists, medical examiners, and **criminalists**) would analyze any evidence they gathered, not the CSIs. (Occasionally CSIs can function in multiple roles as Grissom and his team do, but usually only in smaller cities or towns where low crime rates, limited personnel, and poor funding are the norm.)

Remember, *CSI* supposedly focuses on what lead detective Jim Brass calls the "second-best crime lab in the nation." You would think it better staffed than most. Yet Gil Grissom and his team seem to do it all: gathering evidence at the scene, documenting evidence, photographing or sketching crime scenes—all accurate tasks for CSIs—as well as personally running the scientific tests (on corpses, bones, soils, body fluids, bugs, toxins, wounds, fibers, firearms, prints, tracks, etc.) usually reserved for multiple forensic scientists, other specialists, and technicians. This is where *CSI* fails to depict reality.

Additionally, Grissom (and company) interrogate witnesses, notify families, and chase down suspects. In the real world, that would never happen. Those tasks are police work. Lead detectives would rarely, if ever, give CSIs the freedom and authority that Grissom and his team enjoy.

Here's another example. In "Friends and Lovers" (episode 105, the first season's fifth episode), Gil Grissom wants to get a mold of a suspect's teeth and compare it to a bite wound on the deceased's arm. The segments that show making the mold solidly illustrate forensic odontology. They're pretty accurate, but Gil ultimately conducts the comparison to the wound (the forensic odontologist's job), repeatedly questions the victim's best friend (a detective's job), tracks down and questions other witnesses (a detective's work), and ultimately reveals the boy's innocent **culpability** to him (more police work).

The other crime series fail in similar ways. Each takes enormous creative license to enrich characters, heighten drama, and squeeze crime, crime-

TV Transgressions

We've all seen it. In order to avoid altering trace evidence on the outside of a handgun, a television detective lifts the weapon by sticking his pen or pencil down its barrel. In real life, no good detective would do that. Forensic experts often find vital clues in the barrel. Sticking any object inside it before analysis could destroy or change revealing marks. Besides, it's dangerous!

solving, and in some cases, trials and verdicts into limited air time. What better way to develop characters (and our attachment to them) than to have them involved in every process? What better way to fit a time slot than to simplify complex procedures and limit lengthy processes to the results? Viewers don't seem to mind.

TV Movies

Made-for-television movies have the luxury of added time; they usually span ninety-minute to two-hour time slots. But that doesn't mean their depictions of crime and investigation are any more accurate than those of other programs. In fact, these movies are often less accurate, preferring character development and melodrama to glimpses into forensics, or complying with obvious biases over objectivity in order to obtain first broadcasting rights.

Only the most sensational crimes become TV movies. As we covered in chapter 2, certain crimes become "sensational" for a reason, and those

TV movies neatly condense messy true-crime tales into a plot easily solved in a short time span.

reasons spike ratings. The more horrific a crime, the more innocent a victim, the more unlikely a culprit, the more puzzling the motive—the more sensational the case. The trials of Lizzie Borden, Leopold and Loeb, and Bruno Hauptmann are great examples. Each crime took place over seventy-five years ago, yet their details still grab us and hold our attention today.

Current crimes seem to be just as gripping. NBC's controversial *The Burning Bed* (starring Farrah Fawcett) broke new ground in 1984 when it graphically portrayed the case of an abused wife who, in a desperate attempt to escape her husband's brutality, set his bed ablaze as he slept.

According to Court TV, it became the highest-rated made-for-TV movie in history at the time.

All three major networks rushed into movie production when lurid details surrounding Amy Fisher's 1992 shooting of Mary Jo Buttafuoco made the news. Two even aired the same night. Clearly ABC, NBC, and CBS expected viewer interest. America didn't disappoint them.

The 1997 arrest of Mary Kay Letourneau for statutory rape of her then-sixth-grade student Vili Fualaau offered all four elements of extraordinary crime: a married, thirty-four-year-old, elementary-school teacher with four children (unlikely culprit); a twelve-year-old boy whom the teacher had known since he attended her second-grade class (innocent victim); sexual intercourse with a child (horrifying crime); and no idea why this "normal" mom would throw away her job, husband, and kids to have an affair with a child (puzzling motive). After two prison sentences and two babies fathered by the victim, Letourneau became one of the most notorious criminals in Seattle's history. USA's *Mary Kay Letourneau: All American Girl* didn't hurt that fame.

Sometimes in a rush to be first, networks will air a true-crime movie before the story's end. USA's *Perfect Husband* aired over six months before jurors found Scott Peterson guilty of his wife's murder. The jury announced the sentence in December 2004; USA's video had been out since the previous June. The Lifetime network especially seems to love these "true-life" stories; they routinely run three or four a day!

Television executives would not air TV movies if they weren't popular—and these productions are certainly well watched, despite the facts not being as accurate as in other venues we've examined. Producers also tend to exaggerate characters, the slant is often biased, and dialogue is frequently melodramatic. And yet, as with soap operas, millions tune in.

Other viewers, though, prefer the cold, hard facts.

Armchair Investigators: Crime on Television

CASE STUDY:
1892, LIZZIE BORDEN

Police accuse, imprison, and try a Fall River spinster for the axe murders of her father and stepmother. The New England town divides over her guilt or innocence. Eventually the jury acquits her, but questions surrounding the woman and the crime linger for decades. In 1974, William Blast's TV movie *The Legend of Lizzie Borden* (starring Elizabeth Montgomery) greets a captivated public. Blast gives Lizzie a distinct eeriness. The movie is as popular as it is controversial.

On Location

If true-crime shows, forensic dramas, or made-for-TV movies aren't real enough for you, there's always live TV. News programs routinely broadcast footage "on location," some of which is brutal. Coverage of war, police chases, and riots usually offers graphic images, but perhaps the most unsettling examples come from recent crimes: the live airing of a politician's suicide, police brutalizing Rodney King, an angry mob beating an innocent truck driver, the beheading of political hostages by extremists, and more than one network's decision to show victims jumping to their deaths from the World Trade Center during the September 11 tragedy.

Criminal acts and the events they trigger surround us. Sometimes we watch them as they unfold, and sometimes producers dramatize them for effect. In either case, we can't seem to get enough of crime on television. And our fascination extends to the silver screen as well.

exclusive

celebrity

celebrity

4

Criminal Capers: Crime and Hollywood

In 1888, from August to November, five prostitutes from an impoverished district in London, England, are murdered and horribly mutilated. The killer gave himself the nickname "Jack the Ripper." Suspects range from doctors to a schoolmaster, from the Duke of Clarence to a shoemaker. Even the physician to the Royals is suspect. Authorities fail to catch the culprit, and the killings cease as mysteriously as they started. Since the days of silent movies (a mere thirty-five years after these slayings), numerous filmmakers have attempted to translate these crimes into celluloid. Over eight decades, at least a score of movies have spun theories about Jack the Ripper, each incorporating its own degree of detail. *From Hell*, the latest film to chronicle the exploits of Jack the Ripper, opened in 2001. Each film is consistent with bare, known facts, but nearly all the movies capitalize on the savagery and mystery surrounding whodunit.

From 1896 to 1918, two notorious outlaws and their gang of thieves terrorized banks and railways in Idaho, Utah, South Dakota, Wyoming, New Mexico, and Nevada. When the law closed in, the pair escaped to South America, where they either died or faked their deaths only to return to America under false identities. In either case, Robert Redford and Paul Newman forever immortalized the duo in the 1969 classic *Butch Cassidy and the Sundance Kid.* In it, the criminals are the protagonists. They are as likable as they are handsome, and the audience ends up rooting for the "bad guys." Clearly the movie romanticizes Western outlaws, and in its dramatic climax gets the facts wrong.

In reality, Butch Cassidy was a brutal bank robber, but Hollywood depicted him as a handsome and likable cowboy.

In 1906, authorities arrest, try, and convict Chester Gillette for beating and drowning his pregnant girlfriend. Nearly fifty years later, in 1951, A Place in the Sun (starring Montgomery Cliff, Shelley Winters, and Elizabeth Taylor) hits the big screen. In this film adaptation of a true crime, writers portray the murderer and his "other woman" as Romeo-and-Juliet-like characters while villainizing victim Grace Brown. Filmmakers portray Gillette's pregnant girlfriend as a desperate, whining, selfish, and demanding woman; his mistress is portrayed as a supportive, compassionate, and clearly more desirable lover. Gillette is the underdog, a rising star tragically trapped by the poverty of his roots. The victim represents his poverty, and the "other

Film adaptations of real events often bend the truth to portray more sympathetic characters or a more compelling story.

woman" represents his means of rising above it. The license writers take with these characters is generous. You feel sorry for the murderer, angry at the victim, and frustrated with circumstances that lead to what you perceive is the killer's only way out. Yes, the movie depicts an actual crime from the turn of the century, but its makers clearly chose melodrama over truth and took enormous liberties in developing the characters. Their strategy works. *A Place in the Sun* earned nine Academy Award nominations and won six.

In 1931, Prohibition Bureau investigators bring down one of Chicago's most notorious bootleggers, the climax of two years of intensive teamwork. After losing over $1 million worth of illegal breweries to the bureau, gangster Al Capone unsuccessfully tries to bribe those responsible: Eliot Ness, the lead investigator, and two of his team members. All three throw the money back at him—literally. The news media carries the story of the men's incorruptibleness and dub Ness and his team "The Untouchables." The federal government ultimately charges Capone with twenty-two counts of tax evasion and over five thousand counts of violations to the Volstead Act (prohibition). After Capone is found guilty, the courts impose an eleven-year sentence. Thirty years later, in 1987, Paramount releases *The Untouchables* (starring Kevin Costner). This movie honors the heroic work of Ness and his team. Although dialogue in the movie is fictional, most critics agree that Costner's portrayal of Ness is accurate and basic facts are true. Yet the movie takes incredible creative license in a noble attempt to pay tribute to a noble man. It becomes the good-triumphs-over-bad movie of the year.

Four actual crimes, four subsequent movies. In each example, filmmakers chose to approach known facts from specific, strategic angles.

Directors have long used the film industry to move the masses. Notable examples include *Boomerang* (1947), a subtle commentary on political corruption; *10 Rillington Place* (1970), the case that led to the abolition of the death penalty in England; *Midnight Express* (1978), a scathing view of human rights abuses, particularly in foreign prisons; *Breaker Morant* (1980), an incisive courtroom examination of moral ambiguity inherent in war; *The Thin Blue Line* (1988), a documentary that successfully argued the wrong man was convicted for murder by a corrupt Texas justice system; *JFK* (1991), a lengthy exposé of conspiracies (real or imagined) surrounding the assassination of John F. Kennedy; and *Bowling for Columbine* (2002), a documentary examining gun violence. Each of these movies depicted factual crimes, and each stirred thousands using whatever means they could.

Whether retelling crimes of passion, cold-blooded murder, drug running, or robbery, Hollywood knows how to package truth for dollars. The more dramatically or sensationally it wraps facts, the more tickets it sells, and that means money. Additionally, the more controversial a stance, the more media attention. And the more the media attention, the more publicity the film gets, which translates into wider audiences for profit or preaching. Whatever the motives, crime depicted in movies varies widely in accuracy.

Stretching the Truth

In 2002, almost twenty-five years after the release of *Midnight Express*, director Oliver Stone admits to reporters, "It's true I overdramatized the script." He publicly apologizes to the country of Turkey, its people, and its penal system.

Hollywood Horrors

Here are a few common blunders that true detectives might consider Hollywood Horrors:

- an exact time of death (In real life, medical examiners estimate a time of death and usually provide a window of time that is hours long.)
- untraceable poisons (There are no such things! Forensic toxicologists can trace virtually any chemical or its metabolites with time, effort, and the right equipment.)
- instant deaths (Almost no one dies instantly from a gunshot wound or stabbing, and no one goes down with just one punch!)
- sterile or pretty deaths (Real deaths from crime are neither sterile nor pretty.)
- instant lab results (The results of any forensic testing takes days, if not weeks or months to obtain, not a few celluloid moments.)

Less Noble Motives

Movie writers and directors get paid to create drama—that's their job. To create intensity, retelling criminal cases often becomes one-sided and emotionally charged. But based on a study of moviegoers, the average viewer doesn't enter a theater to sit through a political or moral diatribe. Most moviegoers go because the stories are mysterious or horrifying. Whether or not we admit it, there's something primitively satisfying about being simultaneously absorbed and repulsed, and attracted and repelled—a fact that is not lost on directors.

Look at *From Hell* (2004), *Compulsion* (1959), and *The Boston Strangler* (1968). Each one of these films, while remaining remarkably true to recorded facts of real murders, commonly preyed on a universal base fear: leaving this earth by the cruel hands of another. Yet we can't help being curious about the hands that kill the innocent. Like Clarice (Jodie Foster) in *Silence of the Lambs*, we naively believe we can learn something about ourselves—or at least human nature—by looking into the heart of a killer. And it thrills us.

Controversial movies attract media attention, which, in turn, attracts movie-goers.

Criminal Capers: Crime and Hollywood

Romanticism

One genre of true-crime movies seeks not to preach, thrill, or scare but to romanticize crime or the criminal. *Butch Cassidy and the Sundance Kid* (1969), *A Place in the Sun* (1951), and *Bonnie and Clyde* (1967) are good examples. In all three cases, the movies include actual facts in skeletal form, but creators chose to soften culprits' personalities to the point that those on the wrong side of the law emerge as protagonists. The victims become loathsome and somehow to blame.

Directors love creating an underdog. They know audiences will cheer for anyone they see as oppressed—even brutal murderers—because they somehow identify with the seeming injustices these characters face. Consequently, calculating killers evolve into likable, even sympathetic villains with a wave of the director's hand. But one fact remains: they committed crimes.

This is true of fictional crime movies like the *Ocean's Eleven* series (2001, 2004, and 2007) and *The Italian Job* (2003). Hollywood sends us mixed messages when they portray criminals as cool, attractive, witty, humorous, smart, sexy, and even likable. Most criminals are nowhere near that engaging. Their opponents—be they the law or other criminals—are usually not as stupid, clumsy, or corrupt as writers make them out to be, and the majority of crimes are not nearly as fun.

Heroism

Sometimes movies depict real crimes to honor true heroes. We see such treatment in *The Untouchables*. The uncompromising Eliot Ness and his team of nine detectives gather an astounding amount of evidence under life-threatening circumstances and take down a notorious 1930s crime lord, Al Capone. An autobiographical account by Ness is the basis for the movie.

CASE STUDY:
WAS COUNT DRACULA A WOMAN?

In a 1609 town, officials charged a fifty-something Hungarian countess with eighty counts of murder after finding dozens of female corpses in and around her castle. Investigators found disfigured survivors too, imprisoned in basement dungeons. Records show that witnesses attested to three hundred or more victims, and a written list kept by the countess identified over 650 of the bodies. All victims were young and attractive, each repeatedly cut, pierced, and beaten, and every corpse was drained bloodless. Why? Countess Erzsébet Báthory believed that using young women's blood as a skin moisturizer preserved youth. She was convicted and died, walled in isolation a few years later. In 1744, a Catholic priest published the first formal account of these events, which inspired tales of vampirism. Many historians believe Bram Stoker, while influenced by Vlad the Impaler, chose to set his 1897 novel *Dracula* in Transylvania as a result of Báthory's crimes. One hundred years later, countless movies depict female vampires as temptresses looking for eternal youth. Most combine sensuality with gore in clearly fictionalized accounts of a true serial killer.

Did a man named Eliot Ness really take on the mob? Yes. Was he as unassuming a hero as Kevin Costner makes him out to be? Again, apparently yes. Did the dialogue and action transpire as scripted? Historians say not even close. But apparently in filmdom, that's okay. Basic facts are present and accurate, and the public gets to cheer for true-life heroes. It's a win-win.

Just the Facts, Please

Perhaps less common of all approaches to cinema crime is the one in which a director intends to reiterate the facts and let the viewer decide what's true or just. Three examples of this genre come to mind: *Compulsion* (1959), *The Boston Strangler* (1968), and *The Passion of the Christ* (2004). *Compulsion* recounts the murder trial of Leopold and Loeb (see chapter 1). The crime itself was sensational—the killing of a fourteen-year-old boy purely for sport—but it was Clarence Darrow's courtroom monologues that made this trial ultimately filmworthy in directors' minds. Every word Orsen Welles speaks (as Clarence Darrow) in courtroom scenes is remarkably consistent with trial transcripts. The film simply retells the facts and lets the viewer decide the killers' motives.

About ten years later, director Richard Fleischer recounts the events of a New England killing spree with objective precision in his movie *The Boston Strangler* (starring Tony Curtis and Henry Fonda). The movie is startling in its accuracy, reality, and intensity, particularly for the time when it was released. Fleischer resists the temptation to glamorize anything about the killings. He does, though, choose to believe Albert DeSalvo's confession and clearly portrays him as the killer, although he was never charged with the murders and many, including some of the victims' family members, doubt his guilt.

On a more current note, many critics feel director Mel Gibson accurately re-creates the capture, trial, torture, and execution of Jesus in his movie *The Passion of the Christ*. Others believe Gibson exaggerates events to **proselytize**. In either case, Gibson spares no punches illustrating the brutality of the Roman justice system. Critics argued that the violence depicted in *The Passion* is gratuitous, while many historians claim it is an accurate depiction of historical events, much like the graphic, opening scenes of *Saving Private Ryan* (1998). Accurate or not, Gibson uses the violence to further his ends, creating an emotional view of Christ's death.

Critics accused the filmmakers of *The Passion of the Christ* of using gruesome, violent images.

CASE STUDY:
MYSTERIOUS MOTIVES

In 1924, two brilliant graduate students randomly grab a fourteen-year-old boy, kidnap him, beat him, and mutilate his corpse just for the thrill of it. Less than forty years later *Compulsion* (1959), starring Orson Welles as defense attorney Clarence Darrow, attempts to dissect the psychology of the crime. The movie doesn't question the boys' guilt or innocence; it focuses on defense attorney Darrow. Director Richard Fleischer puts facts to screen and retells a chilling mystery remarkably true to the record. (See chapter 1 for more details of the crime.)

Directors of *Compulsion, The Boston Strangler*, and *The Passion* assert that the uncontested facts surrounding each case were sensational enough to carry their movies. Reality can be as dramatic, if not more so, than fiction. All three films relied on raw events to engage audiences.

Viewing's Many Faces

Criminals, their crimes, and the justice system seem to captivate us as much on the silver screen as on TV or in the news. Crime mysteries—tame or brutal, cerebral or sensorial, accurate or distorted—engage our attention dramatically and often intelligently. Plots challenge us, enrage us, devastate us, and encourage us.

For many of us, stories about crimes are simply an escape from everyday pressures. For others, the idea that crime happens to average, middle-class people unsettles them, and they feel more alert, even more alive. For still others, true-crime characters provide an opportunity to connect with an issue or individual with whom they identify. Last, crime movies, particularly those depicting specifics of an investigation, can be educational. We learn about forensics, interviewing techniques, courtroom strategies, legal processes, and strengths and weaknesses of our justice system.

Mostly we're simply intrigued. Movies about crime let us peek into a world few of us will ever enter. Yet the wide screen is fast losing out to the computer screen. Has our timeless obsession gone electronic? From crime TV websites to legitimate investigative resources, from live video footage to gaming, the business of crime and investigation is just a few keystrokes away.

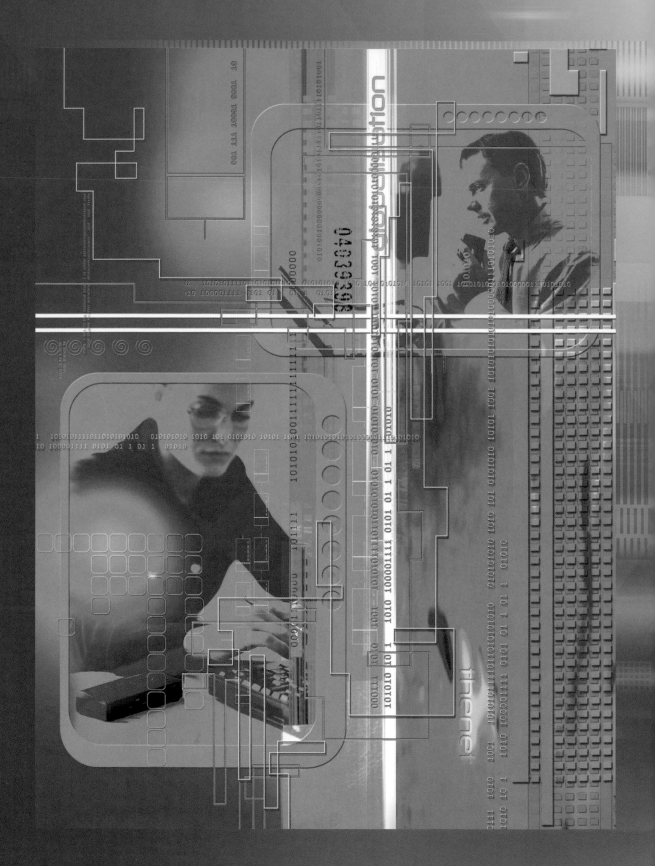

Virtual Villains: Crime and Computers

Crime on the Internet is nothing new. Major networks and news organizations like the Associated Press, the Canadian Press, the *New York Times*, *USA Today*, the *Toronto Star*, and the *National Post* all have websites that cover up-to-date crimes and other news.

Plus the opening page of most Internet service providers (ISPs) and nearly every search engine offers at least one news link, if not a ticker-tape banner for up-to-the-minute news. Consequently, amateur sleuths can track down just about any interesting crime on hundreds of websites worldwide. But availability doesn't guarantee quality.

Keep in mind that when communication vehicles are limited, the process of determining what receives publicity is more selective. The media tends to be more discriminating about what they will publish or broadcast—print, radio, and television alike. But when communication resources are virtually un-limited, as they seem to be today, prioritizing becomes less necessary. An "anything goes" mentality takes hold. This trend seems particularly true of the Internet.

Because it is world wide, the Internet is tough to police and even tougher to censor. Criminal pornographers enjoy the most open market they've had in history. Violent crimes the major networks would never air have entire websites devoted to them and their perpetrators. For example, according to the Associated Press, the gruesome beheading of thirty-three-year-old South Korean translator Kim Sun-Il did not make Al Jazeera TV (or American TV), but video and still pictures quickly made their way onto the Internet. Ter-rorist sites still continue to get hits for the images they display.

On the Lighter Side

Most Internet fans look to satisfy their crime cravings through less extreme fixes. Court TV regularly interacts with its viewers via the Internet. Some-times anchors will solicit viewer feedback, often polling audiences with regard to a suspect's guilt and the admissibility of certain testimony. Not surprisingly, thousands respond electronically to the polls.

The network also provides three main websites: CourtTV.com, CrimeLi-brary.com, and SmokingGun.com. CourtTV.com offers exclusive web con-tent about upcoming programs, a forensics FYI, and even games that re-quire players to apply forensic science knowledge to cases.

CrimeLibrary.com is exactly what the site's name suggests: a crime library. In-depth articles on scores of crimes delight mystery buffs every-where. The library organizes its content into five broad categories: serial killers; gangsters and outlaws; notorious murder cases; the criminal mind; and terrorists, spies, and assassins. A sixth category, "premium content,"

Prison-Cam?

According to *Business Day* (Thailand's first international business daily newspaper), Thailand will soon make Internet video broadcasts of prison life. Cameras have already been installed at Bangkwang Maximum Security Prison outside Bangkok, which houses four thousand inmates. Video coverage will include daily life and even a convict's last moments before execution, but executions will not air. "From now on people can see life in prison through the Internet," boasts Corrections Department Chief Nathee Chitsawang. What do officials hope to accomplish? Less crime.

features a highlighted case or two. Organizers further break down each of the five main archives into various subclassifications, some with intriguing names like "The Truly Weird and Shocking." Tucked among all those dusty articles about past crime, the website flashes a regular "missing child alert."

Fictional shows like *Law & Order* and *CSI* boast websites. *CSI*'s site (www.csifiles.com) provides episode guides for all three *CSI* shows, program reviews, and chat threads where viewers can brainstorm theories and analyze evidence. *Law & Order*'s site (www.nbc.com/Law_and_Order/) offers episode guides and special features like trivia quizzes. These crime-fixes are undoubtedly fun and entertain. But computers and the Internet also meet more serious needs around the world.

A Serious Tool for Serious Work

The criminal justice system and its related but separate branches generate staggering amounts of fact-laden documents. Today, computers and the Internet store and facilitate the retrieval of that information. In the past, records were kept on paper. The simple act of filing the information must have been overwhelming! Can you imagine trying to root through all that information when investigating a case? The advent of the computer greatly simplified that process.

Police, criminalists, and forensic scientists now operate more efficiently and effectively than ever. Files that once took up entire basements (if not buildings) now fit in memory chips typically less than a quarter-inch square. Detectives can track details about a suspect or crime right from their desks. What is even more amazing, field officers can access computers in their patrol cars, right at the scene of a crime, so they can trace, for example, whether a vehicle is stolen or search for outstanding warrants and missing persons.

Obviously the depth, breadth, and immediacy of electronic information make the Internet an invaluable, crime-solving tool. Forensic technicians routinely tap databases worldwide that file millions of fingerprints, tire treads, and fiber samples. The comparative samples they need are often right there, including photo images and videos.

Police computers can access and retrieve countless bits of data from virtually anywhere: sex offender registries; motor vehicle registries; phone records; financial histories; credit card records; ATM logs; missing persons files; birth, death, and marriage certificates; prison records; criminal backgrounds; and lost person sites are just a few examples of what the Internet can make available to an investigation. The miracle is electronic communication.

Inventions and Investigation

Forensic sciences are only as effective and advanced as their counterparts in the scientific community. Here are some milestones from general science that catapulted forensic sciences to new heights:

- the discovery and naming of blood types and the Rhesus or Rh factor
- the invention of the microscope
- the invention of the camera
- the invention of Neuron Activation Analysis, which enabled the identification and measurement of trace elements in a sample of evidence, no matter how small
- the invention of the computer and microchip
- the invention of the Internet
- the discovery of DNA

One such tool is the FBI's National Crime Information Center (NCIC), a huge database that allows law enforcement agencies across the continent to share information, bridging jurisdictions. If, for instance, a gun was a murder weapon in Chicago, NCIC allows an investigator to check its characteristics with **ballistics** evidence from a murder in Seattle or Miami. The information it provides is not only available to law enforcement offices spanning the United States and Canada; NCIC 2000 also extended the service to individual police cars and mobile officers.

Data-sharing has become invaluable to the detective process. Other applications include crime profiling. Detectives can enter facts of a crime into an official search engine, then scan hundreds or thousands of cases from a geographical region to see if any patterns emerge. All of this takes place in a matter of minutes, not days or weeks.

Advocates of privacy laws continue to fight the accessibility of some facts. Remember, even though it's been around nearly thirty years, the Internet is a relatively new tool in crime-fighting, and the medium has stymied lawmakers who are unsure how to regulate it. Many e-supporters believe restricting any information on the Internet constitutes a violation of First Amendment rights. Others believe governments are only steps away from

Internet databases help law enforcement agencies organize information from across the country in one place.

Data Data

According to the Federal Bureau of Investigation, as of 2011, its National Crime Information Center manages an average of 7.9 million inquiries a day!

a "Big Brother" state, like in the George Orwell novel *1984*. These people don't want personal information to be made so readily available and consider it an invasion of privacy. The matter is quite complex, and lawyers will be debating these issues in court for years.

Hidden Threat?

In the meantime, the scope of what's accessible online—a boon to crime buffs—has caused concern among educators. Parents and teachers worry that children can access inappropriate material too easily while innocently searching online. Because of these concerns, many Internet services and soft-ware companies provide programs that prevent "surfers" from inadvertently stumbling into graphic, violent, or offensive material. Organizations like SafePlace and parental control software like Net Nanny are two examples.

If you're a crime junkie and love to surf for the latest mysteries or breaking news, use your head while going online. Great information and mind-bending whodunits exist out there, but be careful about the nature of the details you provide about yourself, especially when making online purchases or using gaming sites. You can never be sure who it is that's getting your information. If someone sends you a violent, vulgar, or offensive message, ignore it and tell a trusted adult. On the other hand, don't ever send violent, vulgar, or offensive messages, regardless of whether you mean them.

Police take Internet threats and even fictional online accounts of crime quite seriously. They're no joke. Consider the case of one college student who penned his fantasy for the entire online community to see. His fictional entry described the rape of a young woman who strongly resembled one of his classmates. Police interrogated him intensely for hours, and the girl was terrified even though the incident never actually took place.

"I" Spy

When it comes to forensics, the Internet offers endless means of satisfying the inner detective. Just type in "forensics" in a popular search engine, and you'll likely get over thirty million results in less than a half second! From research laboratories to the FBI (www.fbi.gov), from the Royal Canadian Mounted Police (RCMP) to universities of forensic sciences, amateur detectives can follow forensic advancements and investigations like never before.

After the tsunami of 2004, the RCMP deployed a team of forensic identification specialists to Asia to help in disaster recovery work there. According to their official website, the RCMP immediately responded with ten forensic specialists whom they sent to Bangkok, Thailand, to identify bodies. The team worked under the guidance of Canada's ambassador to Thailand and Interpol's Disaster Victim Identification Subcommittee.

What did they do there? Check out the site and see! The RCMP Web site details the team's specific tasks and the forensic science it applied to accomplish the work. For example, while specifying procedures for mass

Ten Steps for Internet Sleuthing

1. Be selective about the websites you visit. Ask around.
2. Don't accept everything you see online as truth, even images. Cross-check information and consider your sources.
3. Treat everyone you encounter online as strangers. They really are.
4. Think for yourself. Evaluate everything you see and hear.
5. Skip all violent, graphic, racist, terroristic, and pornographic sites.
6. Never give out home information like your address or telephone number.
7. Never give out your Social Security number.
8. Be cautious about how much you tell others about yourself.
9. Don't respond to threatening, violent, or obscene messages, and never send them yourself.
10. Trust your instincts. Confide in a trusted adult if something concerns you.

victim identification, the site clarifies:

> In the case of a mass disaster, victim DNA identification is performed by referencing similarities in DNA patterns with other biological relatives from the same family or through DNA profiles that are derived

There are innumerable forensics resources that can be found online.

from the personal belongings of a victim. Possible sources of DNA can include hair follicles in a hair brush and toothbrushes.

You can't get more specific than that! Regarding fingerprints, it further warns:

In the case of fingerprints, impressions can be taken and compared against fingerprints stored in various repositories. In Canada, the RCMP is the steward of fingerprint records. Interpol can support comparisons with repositories in other countries, based on agreements that protect the privacy rights of Canadians. Gathering fingerprints from a person who has died can be difficult if the body has begun to decompose.

Hundreds, if not thousands, of similar law enforcement sites float within our virtual world. For forensics buffs everywhere, these sites are like honey to a bear.

What about those who prefer action to lurking? Sites and software abound for aiding slippery sleuths. Net Detective, the detective software endorsed by the National Association of Private Detectives (NAPD), is popular among licensed private investigators, but it is also available to the general public at typical software prices.

If you don't know what you need or where to start, search engines such as Crime Spider's Crime Library (www.crimespider.com) scans the best crime and law enforcement sites, then categorizes select resources by topic. This tool alone can facilitate research on criminalistics, forensic anthropology, homicide investigative techniques, behavior profiling, unsolved murders, missing persons, criminals, serial killers, kidnappers, crime-scene photos, crime statistics, law, and criminal justice to simply name a few. From background checks to locating lost loves, Americans can conduct remarkably extensive investigations of their own.

Over recent previous decades, advances in media communications have exposed the belly of crime-solving to everyday people like us. Innate

The Internet makes satisfying a craving for crime-solving easy.

puzzle-solvers love it! For many, criminal investigation has become a hobby of sorts. For others, the exposure has tickled a longing to pursue the subject in greater depth. For a few more, careers in forensic-related fields await.

6

Criminal Genius: Using Crime in Education and Related Careers

Construction-paper footprints crisscross a polished hallway. Lipstick kisses arch over a science room door. Seventh-graders at this middle school huddle around microscopes, examining fingerprints, blood, and dollar bills.

Forensics is a hot topic. It's already gripped our media and our entertainment. Now, education has fallen in line. Teachers recognize a good hook when they see one.

Actually, according to one middle-school teacher, educators have been using forensics to teach science curriculums for decades, clearly years before the current craze. Why? Forensic science, the sciences we apply to legal matters, intrigues us. Kids are no exception. It's innately human to puzzle-solve.

In the early twentieth century, teachers rarely tied science's foundational concepts, like observation and inference, to any practical application. Instructors would drone on about such methods from their textbooks, boring students to no end. For many, science was dead.

But somewhere along the line, modern educators realized the powerful, attention-grabbing potential in teaching science through forensic applications. Educational publishers soon developed formal forensics curriculums for middle- and high-school students. Such curriculums have proven themselves remarkably effective, piquing new student interest in science—in some, for the very first time. Common use among educators, though, didn't see a dramatic surge until recent years.

Forensics can add excitement to school subjects that might otherwise seem boring.

TV, Meet the Classroom

In 2003, the National Science Teachers Association (NSTA)—the world's largest organization of science educators—teamed up with Court TV to develop exciting forensics-based science curriculums for middle- and high-school students.

According to a 2004 survey conducted by the National Science Teachers Association (NSTA), forensics was the hottest trend in science early in the 2000s, and from the dozens of textbooks, lesson plans, and websites dedicated to teaching students about forensics, it doesn't look like that trend is going away anytime soon. Why the sudden increase in forensics in education? When asked if they thought the popularity of crime-based TV shows spurred student interest in science, 78 percent of teachers replied with a resounding yes. Teachers are simply seizing the opportunity to reach kids.

At Penn Central Middle School in Perkasie, Pennsylvania, seventh-graders learn the concept of proportion by studying footprints. How? Generally the size of an adult footprint represents 15 percent of that person's height. Students at this school also learn about observation skills by examining "kiss prints" under a microscope. "The first thing is to get their attention and hold it," explains middle-school science teacher Chris Potylycki. "Forensics does that very well." So does kissing paper!

How many other science skills or concepts does such a curriculum teach? Certainly more than you can count on two hands. Here is a partial list:

- what is a scientist?
- how to use a microscope
- observation
- how to observe effectively
- data collection
- data analysis
- application and evaluation
- deductive reasoning
- drawing conclusions
- making predications
- documenting results
- communicating results

Additional classroom tools include forensics-based episodes of educational programming like those of *Nature* and *Bill Nye the Science Guy* (usually available on DVD or online). A few television networks offer online resources specifically geared toward educators and their students. One such site is "Forensics in the Classroom" (apps.trutv.com/forensics_curriculum/index.html).

Career-Minded

What about those students who want to move further with such studies? Some school districts now offer mini "police academies" for high-school students considering law enforcement careers. Working with the local police department, these academies usually take place on site at police headquarters. Students learn about the general qualifications, training requirements, and daily responsibilities of law enforcement personnel as they become acquainted with their facilities. Staff members also expose students

If you think you may be interested in a career in forensic science, take advantage of the forensics opportunities offered by your school.

to crime-scene photos, videos of actual crimes, and accident scenes. Many students even get an opportunity to experience an eight-hour tour as they accompany an officer on duty.

Other schools invite officers into their classrooms. These guest speakers cover subjects including law and society, search and seizure, vehicle stops and searches, search warrants, locker searches, effects of alcohol, drinking

Criminal Genius

Dead Definition?

Autopsy literally means "to see for oneself." The first autopsy on record is that of Julius Caesar (44 BCE). What was the cause of death? He died from twenty-three stab wounds.

and driving, canine units, forensic sciences, law enforcement careers, and how to become a police officer. The officers tailor topics to meet classroom needs and student interest.

Beyond High School

Answer these two questions: Do you like science? Do you like law enforcement? If you answered yes to both questions, a career in forensic science may be for you.

The world of forensics is a diverse one. Not only are there many branches of forensic investigation, but to complicate matters, each police jurisdiction has its own way of doing things including varying its job titles and responsibilities depending on budgets, personnel, and facilities. For the sake of simplicity, the job titles and descriptions listed here are general in nature. From conducting autopsies to viewing documents, from profiling criminals to taking dictation, there might be one that intrigues you.

In chapter 3 we showed how much teamwork is really involved in true-crime investigation. No one person handles it alone. Here is a list of the main positions a well-staffed forensic team needs to play the game. Basic job responsibilities follow where needed.

FIRST ON THE SCENE

- Coroner: an appointed or elected official (formerly requiring no medical or forensic skills) who takes charge of corpses and can order autopsies.
- Medical Examiner: a licensed physician (licensed to practice medicine and trained in forensic pathology) who performs autopsies and investigates any unattended deaths and all deaths by violence, suicide, or criminal acts.
- Crime-Scene Investigation Unit (CSIU): trained in spotting, recognizing, collecting, transporting, and preserving evidence.
- Crime-Scene Photographer/Artists: artists who preserve the scene of the crime by shooting it on film from all angles or sketching its details on paper.

CRIMINALISTS

- Crime Scene Investigators: CSIU members who locate, collect, protect, and transport all physical evidence to the crime lab. They are trained to see evidence.
- Latent Print Examiners: specialists who uncover, obtain, and examine fingerprints, footprints, and palm prints and then compare them to print databases or other records.
- Trace Evidence Examiners: specialists who analyze and compare fibers, soils, paints, and hair to determine type and origin.
- Tool Mark Examiners: specialists who identify marks at a crime scene and compare them against suspect tools.
- Firearms Examiners: specialists who search for and identify gunshot evidence such as powder residue, bullet holes, bullet fragments, and shell casings.

- Ballistics Experts: those who specialize in the functioning and unique characteristics of specific firearms and bullet projectiles.

FORENSIC SCIENTISTS

- Forensic Anthropologist: studies human bones to determine the identity of the deceased (gender, age, race, etc.); also examines the circumstances in which the bones were found; may consult on time-of-death issues.

- Forensic Pathologist: a licensed physician trained in pathology (diseases and injury and the functional or structural changes they cause in the human body); is in charge of any bodies and all evidence gathered from examining them; also conducts autopsies; pursues answers using medical records, interviews, and lab evidence.

- Forensic Accountant: conducts financial investigations related to motive or identifying suspects.

- Forensic Botanist: studies plants and plant residue like seeds, spores, pollen, and plant fragments at the crime scene.

- Forensic Chemist: examines molecular attributes of evidence like glass, paint, dyes, chemicals, and even fibers.

- Forensic Criminologist: analyzes crime scenes from a psychological angle to determine potential motives and behavior during the crime.

- Forensic Dactyloscopist: analyzes and compares fingerprints.

- Forensic Document Examiner: examines written and printed materials to identify or confirm age, authorship, and authenticity.

- Forensic Entomologist: studies behaviors and life cycles of insects that feed on corpses to determine location of death and time of death.

- Forensic Geologist: analyzes soil residue to trace where a body or suspect has been.

- Forensic Linguist: examines spoken and written words to assist in identifying or profiling a suspect, crime pattern, or motive.
- Forensic Medical Transcriber: transcribes specialized medical and technical dictation regarding autopsies and other forensic tests.
- Forensic Odontologist: a dentist who studies crime evidence related to teeth (bite marks on bodies or foods, teeth impressions, and dental records for identifying human remains).
- Forensic Profiler: creates a likely profile of an unknown suspect (age, race, gender, lifestyle, employment, family history, etc.) based on comparative evidence from serial crimes; can sometimes predict what a serial offender will do.
- Forensic Psychiatrist: assesses witnesses, determines suspects' sanity and competence to stand trial; conducts psychological autopsies on suicide victims; may also be involved in behavioral profiling.
- Forensic Serology: analyzes body fluids like blood, saliva, and semen related to crime to determine DNA, blood type, race, and even parentage.
- Forensic Toxicologist: studies drugs and poisons in both the living and dead to assess causes of aberrant behavior or death; also examines samples from drunk-driving tests and employee or student drug testing.

What a team! Can you imagine winning a football game without your quarterback, kicker, punter, receivers, tackles, or tight ends? How about without your coach or even the equipment manager? Each member of a football team is vital to the team's success. The same is true of forensic investigation teams.

Everyone has their niche. Every team member contributes a skill or talent for which they've specifically trained and at which they're quite good.

Criminal Genius **103**

Pocket Pal

One of the earliest documented accounts of forensics in action was the 1784 English case of John Toms. A torn piece of newspaper found in his pocket matched newspaper a murderer used to pack gunpowder in a murder weapon. Mr. Toms was convicted.

Some players have to train for years to accomplish their skills while others require less to hone theirs. Training for forensics careers varies as widely.

Some forensics jobs only require a strong interest in the field to break in. Others require a medical degree. Many require board certification, while still others have no certification requirements at all. One prerequisite, though, is true of every position: you can't have a criminal record. By definition, forensics deals with matters of law, and to work in law enforcement you can't have a rap sheet.

If any of these positions intrigue you, find out more about them. Other books in this series explore select fields in much greater depth. Or check online resources, related technical institutes, and local colleges. You can even visit law enforcement agencies. (Many host open houses.) Doing your homework can clarify what is required for any given field and where you can obtain those requirements.

The Initial Call

Way back in 1910, across the Atlantic Ocean in Lyons, France, an unassuming police officer named Dr. Edmond Locard had a thought. The revolutionary detective theorized that "every contact leaves a trace." He further believed that such knowledge could solve crime. Locard proved both when he scraped beneath a suspect's fingernails and found flakes of skin covered with his victim's face powder.

The Locard Principle, as his theory became known, is the basis for modern forensic investigation. It basically asserts that every contact a person makes with another person, animal, object, or place results in an exchange of matter. Look at your collar; chances are a piece of hair is clinging to it. Examine your socks; if you have a pet, there's sure to be animal fur stuck to them. See what's on the bottom of your shoes or under your nails.

Wherever we go, we leave a little bit of ourselves behind—and in turn, we pick up bits of other people, places, and things. Finding out who, what, when, where, how, and why (as it relates to crime) is what forensic sciences are all about. Opportunities to be detectives exist every day, everywhere, if only we could train our eyes to see.

Glossary

aberrant: Deviating from what is normal.

ballistics: Having to do with the firing, flight, and effects of firearms or ammunition.

carbines: A lightweight rifle with a short barrel.

carnage: A massive slaughter or massacre.

celluloid: The material used to make motion picture or photographic film.

clique: A highly exclusive group.

criminalists: Persons who specialize in the collection and examination of physical evidence in a crime.

coroner: A public officer who investigates any death thought to be of other than natural causes.

culpability: Blameworthy; being wrong or evil.

culvert: A covered channel that carries water or cabling underground.

deadlocks: Unable to reach a decision.

desensitization: The process of becoming emotionally unresponsive or unaffected by something through long exposure or repeated shocks.

macabre: Related to death, horror, or decay.

minutiae: A small or trivial detail.

niche: A position particularly well suited to a person.

privy: Aware.

proselytize: To convert someone's religious or political beliefs to your own.

psychopaths: People with an antisocial personality disorder who may exhibit aggressive, perverted, criminal, or amoral behaviors without empathy or remorse.

stereotyping: To make oversimplified generalizations about a group or a person belonging to a specific group, often based on incomplete and inaccurate information.

sterilize: To make something unoffensive.

vicariously: To experience something through the actions of another person.

Further Reading

Blanche, Tony, and Brad Schreiber. *Death in Paradise: An Illustrated History of the Los Angeles County Department of Coroner.* New York: Four Walls Eight Windows, 1998.

Camenson, Blythe. *Opportunities in Forensic Science. New York: McGraw-Hill, 2009.*

Campbell, Andrea. *Forensic Science: Evidence, Clues, and Investigation.* Philadelphia, Pa.: Chelsea House Publishers, 2000.

Evans, Colin. *The Casebook of Forensic Detection: How Science Solved 100 of the World's Most Baffling Crimes.* New York: Berkley Trade, 2007.

Genge, Nyaire E. *The Forensic Casebook: The Science of Crime Scene Investigation.* New York and Toronto, Canada: Ballantine Publishing Group and Random House of Canada Limited, 2002.

Gerdes, Louise I., ed. *Media Violence: Opposing Viewpoints.* San Diego, Calif.: Greenhaven Press, Inc., 2004.

Lyle, D. P. *Forensics for Dummies.* Hoboken, N.J.: Wiley Publishing, Inc., 2004.

Morton, James. *Catching the Killers: A History of Crime Detection.* London, England. Ebury Press, 2001.

Ramsland, Katherine. *The Forensic Science of CSI.* New York: Berkley Publishing Group, 2001.

Zonderman, Jon. *Beyond the Crime Lab: The New Science of Investigation.* New York: John Wiley & Sons, Inc., 1999.

For More Information

Federation of American Scientists
www.fas.org

National Crime Information Center
Criminal Justice Information Services (CJIS) Division
www.fbi.gov/about-us/cjis/ncic

Court TV
www.courttv.com

Crime Library
www.crimelibrary.com

Crime Spider Crime Library
www.crimespider.com

Federal Bureau of Investigation
www.fbi.gov

Pennsylvania State Police
www.psp.state.pa.us

Royal Canadian Mounted Police
www.rcmp-grc.gc.ca

United States Department of Justice
www.usdoj.gov

Publisher's note:
The websites listed on these pages were active at the time of publication. The publisher is not responsible for websites that have changed their addresses or discontinued operation since the date of publication. The publisher will review and update the website list upon each reprint.

Index

Picture Credits

Photos.com: pp. 15, 16, 19, 22, 26, 36, 39, 40, 45, 57, 62, 68, 69, 73, 77, 86, 88, 90, 92, 96, 99

To the best knowledge of the publisher, all other images are in the public domain. If any image has been inadvertently uncredited, please notify Harding House Publishing Service, Vestal, New York 13850, so that rectification can be made for future printings.

Biographies

AUTHOR

Jean Ford is a freelance author, writer, award-winning illustrator, and public speaker. Internationally recognized, her work includes writing for periodicals from the United States to China, and speaking to audiences from as close as her tri-state area to as far away as Africa. Although she generally writes and speaks on nonfiction topics, Jean also enjoys writing and illustrating children's books.

SERIES CONSULTANTS

Carla Miller Noziglia is Senior Forensic Advisor for the U.S. Department of Justice, International Criminal Investigative Training Assistant Program. A Fellow of the American Academy of Forensic Sciences, Ms. Noziglia served as chair of the board of Trustees of the Forensic Science Foundation. Her work has earned her many honors and commendations, including Distinguished Fellow from the American Academy of Forensic Sciences (2003) and the Paul L. Kirk Award from the American Academy of Forensic Sciences Criminalistics Section. Ms. Noziglia's publications include *The Real Crime Lab* (coeditor, 2005), *So You Want to be a Forensic Scientist* (coeditor, 2003), and contributions to *Drug Facilitated Sexual Assault* (2001), *Convicted by Juries, Exonerated by Science: Case Studies in the Use of DNA* (1996), and the *Journal of Police Science* (1989). She is on the editorial board of the *Journal for Forensic Identification*.

Jay Siegel is Director of the Forensic and Investigative Sciences Program at Indiana University-Purdue University, Indianapolis and Chair of the Department of Chemistry and Chemical Biology. He holds a Ph.D. in Analytical Chemistry from George Washington University. He worked for three years at the Virginia Bureau of Forensic Sciences, analyzing drugs, fire residues, and trace evidence. From 1980 to 2004 he was professor of forensic chemistry and director of the forensic science program at Michigan State University in the School of Criminal Justice. Dr. Siegel has testified over 200 times as an expert witness in twelve states, Federal Court and Military Court. He is editor in chief of the *Encyclopedia of Forensic Sciences*, author of *Forensic Science: A Beginner's Guide and Fundamentals of Forensic Science*, and he has more than thirty publications in forensic science journals. Dr. Siegel was awarded the 2005 Paul Kirk Award for lifetime achievement in forensic science. In February 2009, he was named Distinguished Fellow by the American Academy of Forensic Sciences.